How to be a Great Boss: A Guide for New Leader

Anthony B. Brown

All rights reserved. No part of this publication may be reproduced,distributed,or transmitted in any form or by any means,including photocopying,recording,or other electronic or mechanical methods,without the prior written permission of the publisher,except in the case of brief quotations embodied in critical reviews and certain other non commercial uses permitted by copyright law.

Copyright © Anthony B. Brown, 2022

Table of Content

[Chapter 1](#)
[Chapter 2](#)
[Chapter 3](#)
[Chapter 4](#)
[Chapter 5](#)
[Chapter 6](#)
[Chapter 7](#)
[Chapter 8](#)
[Chapter 9](#)
[Chapter 10](#)

Chapter 1

Meaning Of The Word "Boss"

Why do we refer to our superiors as bosses, and how did this word come to be used in common speech?
According to Jonathan Haeber, the term "boss" is derived from the Dutch word "baas," which means "master." By using it, Americans avoided using the word "master," which by the middle of the 19th century had fast come to be linked with slavery.

Have you ever heard the saying, "My boss is a slave driver"? Pay attention to the phrases "slave" and "driver." Because they disliked using the term "master," many employees in those days preferred to refer to their superior as "boss." But despite all of their attempts to mainstream the word's usage, they were ineffective since its meaning remained unchanged.

The usage of the terms "boss" and "leadership" interchangeably irritates me because they are quite different, as demonstrated by Lolly Daskal:

A leader is interested in fostering the growth and development of others; a boss is not.

A boss claims the glory; a leader acknowledges others.

The leader says, "Let's go," whereas the boss commands, "Go!"

A boss orders; a leader coaches people to succeed at their highest level.

A boss instills anxiety; a leader arouses excitement.

A boss places blame on others, but a leader strives to fix the harm and figure out what went wrong so it won't happen again.

A boss just thinks about themselves; a leader only considers the group as a whole.

A leader demonstrates how it's done; a boss understands how it's done.

A boss relies on their power; a leader relies on the team as a whole and mutual trust and accountability.

It's simple to use fear as a motivator; all it takes is a little intimidation to persuade someone to work an additional shift, complete an immoral assignment, or make a change that has nothing to do with the organization's mission, vision, or values. When you decide to be a leader, you become someone who values people, uses influence to motivate others to go above and beyond, is a great communicator and can establish connections with individuals at all levels of the organization, and looks out for the interests of others both on and off the field.

There are already enough managers in the world that primarily care about themselves, so you don't need to search very hard to notice that. But since great businesses are aware that incredible things can be done when great leadership is present across the whole organization, many organizations will have no choice but to step up into leadership as the time's change.

Chapter 2

Being a Fantastic Boss

Not everyone is adept at being a good boss. But the majority can relate to a tale about going through a horrible one.

I've heard gruesome tales of abusive managers who would yell at staff members or berate them in front of other people.

Employee morale is severely damaged by this kind of conduct, which also negatively impacts productivity (at least while the supervisor isn't watching).

Employee disengagement caused by poor morale adds to unnecessary stress. When dealing with a poor boss, employees see the culture as "us" vs "them."

These unfriendly workplaces not only reduce worker productivity but are also incredibly difficult to control.

Why not make an effort to build a workplace that promotes enjoyment and fosters productivity given that we spend a third of our life with our coworkers and employees?

Successful managers have worked out what it takes to inspire and motivate staff members. Not everyone knows how to be the boss. So what attributes do outstanding bosses possess?

Here are 10 characteristics of an excellent boss.

1. Expresses a Clear Vision
When employees go to work, they want to excel and make a difference.

Employers are more engaged when their bosses can clearly articulate the organization's goal and assist them to comprehend why they do what they do.

This engages staff members and piques their interest in supporting the organization's goals.

2. Relates vision to routine tasks

The best managers show how the goals of the company are supported by the work performed by their staff.

This is accomplished by drawing a direct link between the employee's daily activities and how they further the organization's goal.

Writing clever objectives that complement organizational goals, which are ultimately connected to company strategy, achieves this.

3. Establishes Specific Performance Expectations

According to research, when workers are unclear about their responsibilities, their stress levels tend to rise.

Provide the individual with a very detailed work description that outlines all anticipated responsibilities and includes employee objectives to establish clear performance expectations.

These expectations should be discussed in-depth in a one-on-one meeting with the employee's supervisor.

Continue to convey updated expectations when priorities shift so that the employee has constant knowledge of their position and duties.

4. Offers Regular Coaching and Feedback
Feedback on how well they are fulfilling expectations must be given often to employees.

Help them recognize their successes and let you know when they fall short of expectations.

Regular coaching of workers may help to accomplish this.

Mention whatever they are doing well if you notice it. Mention anything that needs to be changed as soon as you see it.

Employees often are not even aware that they are not fulfilling criteria. The manager must mentor and help them grow.

When they are not upholding customer service standards, the employer has to let them know.

For instance, if management overhears staff being impolite to a client over the phone, they should call it out and teach the staff how to speak politely to consumers.

The client experience will suffer if this doesn't happen, and the employee may not even be aware that their behavior is improper.

5. Shows concern for the worker as a person
Employees want a sense of personal concern from their employers.

An excellent manager will take the time to find out about an employee's personal life and activities outside of work.

When the employer shows interest in the employees' families, interests, or hobbies, the workers feel appreciated.

Just ask an employee about their children to watch their face light up!

6. Talks about their own experiences
Employers are more likely to respect managers who are vulnerable and willing to share personal experiences with them.

A supervisor may act as a life mentor for staff members by opening up about their troubles and how they deal with problems in life. This not only humanizes their connection.

An extra teaching opportunity arises, for instance, if a supervisor discusses a disagreement they had with a neighbor and how they addressed it.

Additionally, it provides the worker a window into their boss's private life.

7. Adds Fun to Work
If you're not enjoying your job, you're in the wrong one, a manager once told me.

I wasn't sure what he meant at the time, but looking back, it all makes perfect sense.

Every workplace has the potential to be an enjoyable and effective place to work, whether you're flipping hamburgers, serving customers at the front desk, or working a production line in a factory.

Giving staff something to look forward to by including enjoyable activities, events, and planned downtime.

basic things like blue jeans A video game challenge on Friday or during lunch may be not only entertaining but also a fantastic team-building activity.

8. Promotes the Growth of Teams
Team relationships may be challenging because of diverse personalities and frames of reference.

Good team leaders who support team growth are great bosses.

A good leader can rally the soldiers and lead them all in unison in the same direction.

9. Employee Perspectives on Values

Employees carry out the tasks necessary to run a business, and exceptional managers are interested in their opinions and actively seek out their input.

They are aware that many operational issues may frequently be solved by staff.

Employees also cherish the opportunity to share their ideas and views when requested.

10. Honors Outstanding Performance
Employees should be rewarded for fulfilling and going above and beyond job standards since they come to work intending to perform a good job.

Identify the top performers and give them incentives for their hard work by developing a payment scheme.

When employees go to work, they want to do a good job, but occasionally their employer gets in the way of that. Bosses may create an atmosphere that employees are proud of and like working in by communicating the organization's goals, outlining how each employee's job contributes to those goals, and allowing workers to take part in problem-solving initiatives.

What kind of a boss are you then?

Chapter 3

Are You Capable

Some individuals are born leaders who like taking charge and helping a business achieve its long-term objectives. But not everyone is suited for management.

Some individuals are born leaders. They like taking charge, motivating others, and advancing a company's overarching objectives. Additionally, the benefits—more money and possibly even an office or expense account—can be alluring.

But not everyone is suited for management. To get the greatest performance out of every person and to manage many duties at once, takes a certain set of abilities. Additionally, managers put in more hours and are subject to stricter accountability requirements.

Here are some pointers to assist you to assess your managerial aptitude.

OWNED OR MANAGED?

Some employees just develop into supervisors during their careers. Others see it as an opportunity to take on new tasks since they are dissatisfied with their existing employment. Some people are promoted before they're ready during hard economic circumstances, which may penalize them.

New York City counseling coach Lynn Berger noted, "It's not simply an increase in income or a better title." Some persons are more suitable for certain obligations and duties than others.

You should first determine if you would be a suitable match for a managerial role if you are interested in applying.

Here are some questions to think about:
What about your work do you love? If you lost the ability to do those jobs, would you be disappointed?

Observe the issues your supervisor faces daily. Do you want to do those tasks? Can you make them any better?

Are you enthusiastic about coaching others? Are you able to communicate clearly? Well-organized? Team-oriented? Patient?

Are you sure of your skills and who you are as a person?

Can you make someone answerable? Could you reprimand or dismiss a worker?

Dea Robinson, 47, has been the practice administrator for the Inpatient Medicine Service in the Denver neighborhood of Englewood, Colorado, since 1998. She oversees a team of five employees.

She enjoys the diversity and difficulty of her profession, which includes attempting to persuade a tough employee to succeed and coaching others.

The basic conclusion, according to Robinson, is that managers must learn how to communicate with and get along with others.

You don't have to be their buddy to get the most out of someone, she said, but you do need to understand what drives them.

CONS AND PROS

An employee has a fantastic chance to advance professionally when they become a manager. When managers are exposed to all facets of a business's operations, they get a wider view. They are compelled to adopt a broad perspective.

Many individuals may be inspired and motivated by such developments. Others, though, can experience stress, particularly if they've just taken up leadership roles.

You will be responsible for hiring, firing, and writing performance reviews as a manager. You will have to cope with the unexpected, such as figuring out how to continue operating the business when staff is absent due to sickness, a family emergency, or bad weather. or if they lose their jobs.

Elaine Varelas, managing partner at the Boston-based career advising company Keystone Partners, says that's the time when managers need to be adaptable and patient.

If you get promoted to management, it's conceivable that you will oversee former friends, coworkers, and even adversaries.

If so, Varelas advised meeting with each person separately as the best course of action. Pay attention to what they have to say, both individually and then as a group. Do your best to gain their esteem.

Some individuals may learn from their errors or develop into effective managers later in their careers if their first attempt at management fails.

People may depend on a multitude of information, including your company's human resources department, seminars, continuing education, and how-to books if they run across roadblocks or feel they need additional training.

CAN YOU RETROGRADE AT ALL?
There are methods to return to what you love if you become a manager and find that the position is not for you.

Instead of waiting for your employers to come to you, Varelas advised finding a method to return to an individual contributor position and approaching your superiors.

Make sure you can articulate why you want a change and why it would be best for the business.

Talking about your relocation and the reasons behind it with the individuals you oversee is a smart decision as they can wind up being your peers once again.

Just a few years ago, Andrew Kuligowski of Sarasota, Florida, was in that circumstance.

The senior software engineer and programmer chose to become a team supervisor because he believed it to be a logical next step in his career and would be a challenge.

His team fluctuated between three and eight programmers plus outside contractors over two years.

By the middle of the second year, Kuligowski recognized he wasn't at ease since his team's performance was dependent upon it. He became increasingly anxious and often woke up in the night worrying whether things were being done correctly. He worried about any mistakes he may have made or things he should have done better.

Kuligowski said he realized that the absence of a team member with the necessary subject-matter knowledge was his largest challenge. He also understood that going back to programming would make him considerably happy.

He persuaded his superiors that a manager could be hired, and he contributed his knowledge to the team to fill the gap.

He rejoined the group, but then accepted a position with another organization as a senior systems developer. He is also involved in a trade organization where he may contribute his skills as a technical writer and conference organizer.

Chapter 4

Delegate and Elevate

For your firm to expand, you need a plan. You're thinking of appointing a manager. Wrong! Instead, decide to elevate and delegate.The Exceptional Method to Save Yourself from BurnoutYou're accustomed to doing everything yourself since you own a small company. You're ready to develop now, but you're blocking your progress:

Have you discovered that despite having successfully developed your creative firm, you're stuck because you're taking on too much yourself?

Have you attempted to enlist assistance but discovered that no one can do the task as effectively as you can?

Are you angry that your company is stuck and unable to expand without you investing a lot of time in it at the same time?

Are you thinking of appointing a manager to operate your company on your behalf? Even so, is that possible?

Learn how the delegate and elevate strategy may free you from the constraints of your company and rekindle your development in this article.

Delegate and elevate are defined.
Delegate and elevate refers to the practice of delegating part of your work so that you have more time to focus on the most crucial tasks for which you are best suited. If you don't do this, your company will keep running into artificial ceilings that you create. It won't fulfill its potential; you'll burn out, and your company won't ever surpass the ceiling.

You've reached the point when your company is stalled. Your time is being consumed by it, but the benefits have remained the same. While searching for methods to open, you are fundamentally telling yourself:

"My company needs a manager," you say.
Many company owners think about hiring a manager to oversee their firm when they are ready to expand. You would have more time with this. You wouldn't be required to do the duties or jobs you find difficult. That trip you've been promised yourself will finally be possible.

It's so alluring that you begin hunting for others who are similar to you. a multitasker who can take on any task and who is quick to seize the initiative.

You cannot employ a person like you
The "employ a manager like me" approach only has one flaw: it's impossible to locate a such person. You are not cloneable.

From your business concept and your enthusiasm, you have created a prosperous company. Along the journey, you have acquired a variety of special skills. Never will two people have precisely the same talents. Additionally, if you hired a "clone," that individual would have all of your flaws and blind spots!

In any case, should you be recruiting only one person? You're thinking of hiring a manager so they can handle day-to-day operations and you can work fewer hours. How long until you feel the same way about your new management as you do now, and want to leave? Because you've begun to expand and take on new clients, you're in a worse position than you are now when the recruiting process restarts.

The alternative to employing a boss is forming a leadership team.
What should you do if employing a manager is not an option? Building a leadership team

with the necessary competencies is the solution. This is the delegate portion of the equation for delegate and elevate. This tactic has several benefits, such as:

Across all of the roles in your organization, you may recruit experts with specialized knowledge.
Because your employees work hard and like what they do, your company grows. You don't suddenly have to take up all the work you used to perform if one person goes.

When you have a group of talented individuals working for you, you have more time to devote to creating and implementing company development initiatives.

To provide excellent management, consider who, not how.
The key to effective company management is to consider "who?" rather than "how?" (An idea fully explored in Dan Sullivan and Benjamin Hardy's book "Who Not How").

Business owners and entrepreneurs often inquire, "How do we do this?" Consider posing the question, "Who can I get to do this?" To elevate, you must make the mental switch from trying to find out how to accomplish everything alone to concentrate on who you will collaborate with.

List every job you complete. You have undoubtedly spent some time thinking about how to do several of these tasks more successfully and effectively. Now, spend 30 minutes determining who might do these duties more effectively:
- What abilities do they require?
- What jobs will they perform?
- How long will they be working?

Never forget that nobody is going to be able to achieve everything. You're not going to. To complete the task you need to get done, you need to create job descriptions that focus on certain abilities.

How to choose the best candidates
By taking into account the following factors, you must determine who you need to recruit and if you made the appropriate choice.

- Would you be open to exchanging some of your money for some of your time?
- Do you spend excessive time on errands that anybody else could do quickly?
- Are there any tasks on your weekly to-do list that you consistently avoid doing?

Once you've decided to add a new team member, you should write procedural manuals for the duties you want the people who fill your available roles to do.

Finding appropriate applicants to create a virtual team is the next stage. There are several freelancing markets available (such as Upwork, for example).

Make sure you have created an interview procedure and interview questions that will assist you to guarantee the individual you pick can do the job you need them to before you start contacting possible applicants.

Do a paid trial run on one specific job or project next. Give them your procedure manuals without fail. If they are a good match, it will be determined by how they perform.

I was astounded by the impact hiring virtual assistants (VAs) made and still makes when it comes to managing my company. I now have a team of five virtual assistants, each with a unique set of abilities that helps me provide better service to my customers and frees up more time for the activities I like.

Elevate: Watch your role change.
You'll start to notice a change in your function in the company as your team grows. You rise beyond regular management

and begin to take the reins. You work on the tasks that you excel at, find enjoyable, and have a significant impact on your company. Your concentration shifts and you no longer experience business overload. You reclaim control over both your life and it.

Do you ever struggle to efficiently delegate? Have you ever thought about how creative delegating can be?

RAISE TO YOUR SPECIAL ABILITY
I collaborated with a leadership team that developed these eight delegation strategies to maximize its special competence.

D – Delegate Trust in oneself and others is a prerequisite for delegation. When you give someone else a job or duty, this is what happens. Delegate has the following synonyms: assign, turn over, transfer, or authorize.

E - Remove It. Is it truly necessary for you or the company to continue doing this task? If it isn't helping, you may just stop doing it completely.

Let It Go, or L. You sometimes need to let go of a project or method. Trying to be flawless or in complete control will only set you and the team behind.

E-Resources from Experts Have you thought about outsourcing? Some resources can do certain jobs more quickly and often for less money than you can if you do it yourself.

G – GWC™. If you don't provide folks with the materials they need to take their position on an accountability chart, you can't delegate. They must be able to get it, want it, and perform the job successfully.

Automate, or A. Could technology speed up the completion of certain activities or projects? Would automating some of your position allow you to work at a higher capacity?

Track It with T. Not knowing if the individual they are assigned to is doing the task effectively causes some executives great anxiety. If we track progress using a scorecard or another kind of seat measurable, we can allocate tasks more successfully.

E – Elevate You may now rise to your special ability after delegating. You are at your most fulfilled and serving the company to the greatest and best of your ability at this time.

5 steps of help :ELEVATION AND DELEGATION
Elevating yourself to your God-given special talents is one of the best strategies to break through the ceiling and reach your goals.

You probably feel a bit stuck and have much too much on your plate if you're like the majority of company owners, entrepreneurs, and leaders. You could think that you should and ought to be getting a lot more done than you are. If so, following these five actions will help you advance:

Step 1: Establish your 100%. Your 100% is the number of hours you can work each week and yet maintain balance. Without responding to this question, you cannot go to the next stage. Progress starts right here. This response is wholly representative of you.

Determine if you are at capacity in step 2 - How long will it take you to do all you need to accomplish correctly? While not fully simple, this computation is crucial. If your response is more than 100% correct, it's time to promote and delegate. So go to step 3.

Step 3: Make a daily activity list. Although it can seem difficult, investing 30 minutes in it will ultimately save you hundreds of hours annually. Make a complete inventory of all activities, large and little, before moving on to step 4.

Create your two columns in step 4 - Step 3: Sort the items from the preceding list into one of two columns. You should write everything you like doing, enjoy doing well, and are outstanding at in column one. You should mention anything from the step 3 list that is still missing in column two. Proceed to step 5 once everything from step 3 is in one of the two columns. (NOTE: Download and utilize our Delegate and Elevate tool for this phase if you truly want to focus on your special skills.)

Step 5: Delegate and elevate - Until you are comfortable inside your 100%, either stop doing or delegate the surplus capacity items in the second column (or the bottom half of the Delegate and Elevate tool) to the people around you. You must work inside your comfort zone as a leader in your company. You will if you focus the majority of your time on "column 1" activities. You owe it to both your business and yourself. You become more useful, have more energy, and are happier as a result, which makes you a lot better leader for your followers.

6 Steps on How to Become a Delegation Boss

Giving up even one of the crucial duties that keep our lives turning every day may seem as comfortable as donating a kidney to those of us with Type A personalities. However, if you're a solopreneur running a flourishing firm, your refusal to delegate may be preventing you from expanding.

Many of the routine daily chores that keep your company running smoothly may be delegated, freeing up your time for more complex ones. You'll have more time to come up with fresh concepts, seek new business prospects, and optimize your company to be the best it can be rather than merely coasting along.

Here are six short recommendations to get you started if you've thought about employing a new employee (or a virtual assistant!) to handle some of your daily tasks.

1. Be Open and Honest About Your Expectations and Fears.
It's OK to acknowledge that delegation causes you anxiety, but don't worry—it will get simpler! The first step is to communicate clearly. Though virtual assistants are capable of a variety of tasks, reading minds is probably not one of them.

Instead of assuming that people are aware of your preferences, express them. Do weekend email deliveries drive you crazy?

Would you rather make text messages than phone calls? Does a certain typeface make you gag? Inform your assistance!

The secret to doing more will be to set and manage expectations at the beginning. Before beginning a job, take the time to define your priorities and make sure you and the other person are on the same page. Don't hesitate to give it a go! Give details about what you want, when you want it, and the precise result you want to get.

2. Hand over one little task at a time.
Start your road toward mastering delegation by giving the least important and time-sensitive activities priority. This approach offers minimal risk and a fantastic chance to test the delegating waters.

Check-in periodically and provide comments throughout this work. Be prepared to initially need to provide more input to assist set your expectations. As each job is accomplished, keep adding more.

Working with a virtual assistant firm in this situation may be quite beneficial. Many virtual assistant firms will enable you to start with only a few hours per week, then increase hours as you get more comfortable delegating responsibilities. This is preferable to employing a part-time or full-time employee and then immediately attempting to fill 20 or more hours per week with chores.

3. Arrange for a Trial Period

Even with a thorough recruiting procedure and everyone's best efforts, sometimes the first assistant you employ simply won't be the ideal match since many factors of personality and working style are difficult to identify in an interview.

Negotiate a one-month trial period to allow both sides time to see how things go before committing, whether you hire an employee or use a third-party service. Plan a meeting to examine what's working and what isn't after a month to determine whether to continue with a long-term relationship.

4. Establish Written Processes

Even while virtual or in-person pieces of training are excellent, you may simply reduce errors and rounds of questions by having as much as you can on paper. And even if the phrase "procedure" may give you a little uneasy feeling, spending the time to put in the hard effort now will save you headaches afterward.

When changes occur or you recruit new staff, having documented processes in place can help your firm develop in the future. Less work tomorrow means more work today.

Rebekah Hardison, our resident expert on operations, loves following protocols. For advice on creating effective processes for the jobs you assign, see her excellent blog.

5. Attempt to Avoid Micromanaging
Everybody has a distinctive way of doing things, so it's possible that your hired assistant won't carry out every duty in precisely the same manner as you do. That in no way implies that they aren't performing their jobs properly. Concentrate on the result rather than the process. Are your expectations met? If so, the little procedure variations can be worth it just to get that job done.

6. Be Receptive to New Concepts
You probably don't have in-depth knowledge of every facet of managing a small company. There are probably still certain aspects of your management approach that may be improved, even if you may have picked up some new skills along the way.

We at DPM deal with a broad range of customers, particularly in the field of digital marketing, so we have firsthand experience with what works and what doesn't in many situations. We may be able to apply what we've learned to assist you to improve your company management and marketing systems if you're unsure about your method in a certain area.

Identify your areas of weakness and think about employing someone with greater expertise there. You may even find more effective methods of doing things that have a long-lasting effect on your organization if you show that you are open to listening to their recommendations.

Delegating effectively requires patience and trust. It will take some time for the employee you hired to grasp what you do and then replicate it. To execute their job properly, that individual needs your trust, which takes time to earn. The skill of delegation, however, may transform your life and your company in extraordinary ways if you're ready to take the risk.

Chapter 5

Accountability in Leadership

Business success depends on accountability in leadership, but many leadership teams recognize that they still have a long way to go in this area.

72% of company executives and HR experts think that responsibility is essential for corporate success, according to a global study coordinated by leadership accountability specialist Vince Molinaro. Only 31% of respondents are OK with the degree of leadership responsibility they see in their businesses, however.

Why is leadership responsibility so critical to the success of the company, and why do so many leaders find it so difficult to maintain accountability?

The remainder of the company will follow the example that the leaders set. Employees feel helpless and lost without responsibility from top-level executives and intermediate managers. To promote team performance, leaders need to develop responsibility, alignment and focus throughout their teams.

However, a lot of businesses lack the cultural framework needed to clearly define what is expected of leaders. Individuals in leadership positions lack a leadership model for which they may be held responsible if the company's expectations for leadership are not clearly stated. At a time when alignment is more crucial than ever for company success, this leads to fragmented leadership.

To complete the loop between strategy, people, and outcomes, businesses require great leadership. Here's how your business can embrace leadership responsibility.

What Exactly Does It Mean for a Leader to Be Accountable?

The importance of leadership responsibility in the workplace is often undervalued yet is a vital part of a positive culture. However, what exactly is a responsible leader and how can they influence company outcomes?

The word "accountability" implies that managers must answer to someone or something. Accountability is measured in a variety of ways. The first is business performance, which is what most businesses value most. However, in addition to being answerable to the workforce, executives must also be responsible for the corporate culture (defined goal, vision, values, and purpose).

Leaders must be dedicated to the company and its employees to be held responsible. To foster trust among team members, they must take their responsibility as people leaders seriously. Accountable leaders make their teams aware of their goals, objectives, and key outcomes (OKRs) clearly and concisely to promote team focus and alignment. When anything goes wrong, they take responsibility for it and give success its due credit.

Accountable leaders also evaluate the amount of responsibility in those under them. For instance, top-level leadership must hold intermediate managers responsible for their dedication to the company's operations, employees, and corporate culture. By dealing with unaccountable executives, they establish expectations for responsible leadership inside the organization.

By training teams to think critically about the requirements of the firm and how they may maximize their contributions, accountable leaders help promote team responsibility. Owning errors is a crucial component of responsibility and the first step in continuing to move ahead while learning from unavoidable missteps.

What Justifies Accountability in Leadership?

For businesses to stay on course, particularly in a dynamic and unpredictable work environment, leadership responsibility is essential. To maintain staff alignment with the corporate plan across the board, there must be strong responsibility at the top.

Accountability for both people and culture is crucial since they both play crucial roles in generating company success. The whole corporate culture suffers from a lack of responsibility, which lowers employee morale and deters them from working hard.

Employees may feel detached and feel that leaders are just there in the name. If people see that leaders are being paid more while failing to keep their teams together and going in the correct direction, they could become resentful.

A well-defined set of tasks and responsibilities should accompany becoming a leader in your organization. Utilize leadership mentorship programs to increase responsibility. To assist keep them on track, middle managers should have a mentor in a higher-level leadership position. Top executives should have a mentor or executive coach to help their personal development.

Your company can only advance when all of its executives are responsible and in alignment.

Three Components of an Accountability Culture
Culture has a significant impact on how leadership is defined and how accountability expectations are established. Strong leadership cultures that promote

accountability must be fostered by leaders. This helps in establishing leadership development expectations.

Here are three crucial components of an accountability culture that you can promote in your business.

1. Solid Corporate Values

All employees should base their decisions on your company's ideals. Ensure that staff members are aware of your company's values and how they apply to their particular positions. To establish and maintain an environment of responsibility, everyone must understand and uphold the company's principles, not just the executives.

Leaders will feel greater pressure to behave following those principles if all workers can see those values being lived out, or when they are not.

2. A Clear Leadership Paradigm

Although many businesses fail to establish clear expectations, leaders require a defined leadership model for which they may be held responsible. They instead anticipate that others will catch up on hidden leadership expectations. However, this often allows leaders to fill in the gaps with their personal experiences, leading to many conflicting conceptions of what constitutes strong leadership within your organization.

Programs for developing leaders should outline what constitutes leadership inside the organization and establish standards for conduct.

3. Team Responsibility
By definition, team accountability depends on establishing clear expectations for team members in terms of workflows, procedures, and output. People are more likely to fulfill or surpass deadlines and improve overall performance for the company when they feel held responsible to others.

High performance will result from accountability activities inside the team, such as clearly defining expectations.

How OKRs Can Encourage Accountability in Leadership

To hold individuals responsible for their job, you need a clear structure. OKRs provide a framework for establishing both corporate and personal objectives. Better accountability is supported by that framework for both leaders and individual contributors.

Running an OKR program requires managers to be deliberate in their goal-setting and open with their team members. Three elements make up OKR governance:

Accountability

Setting OKRs requires two-way communication to promote responsibility.

The corporate strategy and priorities must be established by the executives, but workers should have the freedom to choose their objectives. To guarantee alignment, this calls for a meeting point between the two sides. The responsibility for coordinating the goals of their subordinates with the overarching corporate plan rests with the leader.

Accountability is crucial for learning from the experience of achieving predetermined goals. Leaders need to be able to guide their people through what worked and what didn't, and explain why, after each quarter. To identify issues and address them going forward, everyone involved must be prepared to accept accountability.

Alignment
The process of vertical alignment between people and the company is driven by accountable leaders. However, horizontal alignment is also important. The term

"horizontal alignment" describes alignment between teams or departments.

Document dependencies when you establish OKRs. When a goal is shared among teams or departments that don't typically collaborate, it must be very clear from the start who is in charge of what parts of achieving the goal. To encourage responsibility and to promote greater communication and openness throughout this process, designate a clear owner.

Focus
Without enough concentration and dedication, OKRs won't be accomplished. Before leaders communicate with their staff, organizations must clarify their goals. The second step is for people to commit to their goals, which calls for specifying clear and well-considered important outcomes.

Accountability is crucial in this situation as well: People must feel responsible for their

OKRs, but leaders must set the standard. To ensure that employee goals are being met, think about designing an OKR template. The form should provide OKR ownership so that each employee is aware of their quarterly goals.

By putting individual OKRs in the perspective of the bigger picture, OKR software may assist provide another degree of responsibility. Individuals may stay focused on accomplishing their goals by understanding how their OKRs fit into the bigger company priorities that comprise their ambitions.

6 Cases of Leadership and Accountability
Grandiose strategic exercises are not the only means of measuring a leader's effectiveness. There are several methods for leaders to show responsibility in their actions and everyday activities.

1. Goals

Goals established by accountable executives reflect the objectives of the company. They now have personal responsibility for generating company success. They also encourage their immediate subordinates to have the same feeling of ownership.

Setting specific objectives for oneself and one's colleagues makes it much simpler to measure responsibility.

2. Performance Administration

Accountable managers provide their staff members with helpful performance feedback. They assist in identifying issue areas and collaborate with people to look into their causes. Individual employees are better equipped to maintain their accountability to the team when they are given clear performance goals.

3. Group Building

Accountable leaders provide a positive leadership model for the benefit of the employees and the firm. The traditional team-building exercise is called the "trust fall," but it is neither as useful nor as impactful as integrating team-building exercises into regular work. Make sure each contributor is aware of their part in creating the finished product by periodically reviewing their or duties.

Leaders and team members tread a tight line in team meetings between keeping each other responsible and never shifting blame. Accountability team building establishes clear standards, models effective leadership, and equips groups with the tools they need to overcome setbacks and discover solutions.

4. Trust

Having an accountable leader builds trust. Employees will trust leaders when they demonstrate unambiguous responsibility and act in the organization's and the workforce's best interests.

Leaders at all levels provide measurable examples of excellent conduct by emulating the company's ideals. This fosters trust among team members, who can detect when leaders stray from their intended course and hold them responsible.

5. Integrity

A leader's integrity is compromised by a lack of personal responsibility. You will become a better leader if you conduct yourself honestly since your followers will appreciate and trust you more for it.

True honesty will be obvious to employees when they encounter it. Integrity-driven leaders provide a positive example for their team members and motivate them to behave honestly at work.

6. Communication

Accountability in leadership depends on communication. Transparent leaders communicate openly with their staff. They employ excellent communication to keep informed and identify possible issues. They take ownership of their behavior as well as that of their team.

Establish communication expectations so that staff members are aware of when and how to get in touch with coworkers and managers. Maintain constant communication to identify and eliminate obstacles to excellent performance.

To drive corporate outcomes, promote a transparent culture, and support your team, accountability must be improved. Your business can advance when everyone is on the same page about expectations and goals. Accountability in leadership may help achieve that.

The link between strategy, people, and outcomes is closed by effective, responsible leaders.

The top 10 methods for being a responsible leader are listed above.

To become more responsible, there are various strategies to improve your leadership abilities. While certain abilities come naturally, many leaders train themselves to carry out particular tasks to be responsible for their work and team members. Consider using the following strategies if you want to learn how to be a responsible leader at work:

1. Make objectives clear

Clarity entails outlining the objective and its significance of it. Clarifying project objectives is one step you may take to become a more responsible leader. Setting up clear objectives and the routes to achieving them makes it simpler for people to take responsibility for various activities. You and other staff members may become more responsible if you continue to be transparent about every facet of a goal.

2. Put the future first.

Another strategy to build responsibility is to concentrate on the department's future. Understanding the direction and strategy of the department is one of your responsibilities as a leader. Planning these specifics will make you feel more accountable for your duties and will ensure your team that you are up to the job. Accountability includes both accepting responsibilities for previous behavior as well as making responsible plans for the future.

3. Obtain suggestions.

By getting feedback as regularly as you can, a leader can increase accountability. You may stay responsible for your obligations by using feedback from your staff. If workers notice you fulfilled the duties on your agenda, obtaining comments about your activities might help you prepare even more for the future project. Your objectives may be adjusted with the use of feedback, which can also show you whether a goal regularly benefits the department.

4. Offer sincere commentary
Giving sincere feedback as often as you can is another step you may take to establish yourself as a responsible leader. Giving your staff feedback based on their duties at work might encourage them to continue taking responsibility for their job in the future. The team may learn more about their development and produce greater outcomes with honest comments. Employees may learn to improve the quality of their work over time while accepting responsibility for their actions by regularly giving honest criticism and encouraging constant accountability.

5. Accept responsibility for mistakes and accomplishments
Accepting the accomplishments and failings of a leader is one method to maintain accountability. Employees are more likely to

see your job in an honest light when you accept both excellent and poor performance from yourself. When speaking about matters about the organization, use "we" instead of "I" to promote this sort of responsibility from everyone. Equal responsibility for your acts creates justice, fosters accountability within your department, and shows excellent accountability to others.

6. Become mindful of your workload

Workload awareness should be practiced as often as feasible if you want to become a more responsible leader. The department's overall work accountability may be improved by knowing how much work you and others can manage at certain periods of the year. Leaders must be accountable in several ways, including just taking tasks they can finish. If you assign your work to another employee because you are unable to do it yourself, this might demonstrate that you are aware of your limitations and have faith in your colleague to get the job done.

7. Make sure communication is efficient.
As a responsible leader, make improvements to your communication strategies to promote a pleasant workplace culture. To ensure that subjects are discussed in the right environment, you may establish a variety of communication channels. A leader should think about supporting open communication as much as possible in addition to providing staff with additional opportunities for communication. Maintaining responsibility for particular goals and encouraging accountability among team members may both be accomplished via open communication.

8. Set objectives based on the team's skills.
By being aware of your team's capabilities, you may enhance your leadership responsibility. It is best to assign work to other staff if you can't realistically complete them within a given amount of time.

However, assigning tasks to workers calls for a thorough understanding of team skills. Knowing what each member of your team is capable of shows that you are aware of their talents.

Understanding each employee's talents and present goals will help you both stay responsible for the job you assign to them. You can assign jobs more efficiently if you know their preferences for the work. By doing this, you may demonstrate to your team that you are aware of their abilities and help you reach your objectives more rapidly.

9. Hold several meetings

Hosting numerous meetings is another method that a leader may guarantee accountability. Regular meetings allow you to evaluate current goals, go through incomplete projects, and clarify needs. Each employee may examine their work during meetings to see whether task distribution is a possibility. Meeting minutes that document progress may be used to organize performance reviews, provide answers to inquiries, and provide fresh perspectives to project advances. By regularly checking in on each other's work, you are embracing responsibility for your actions as well as the team's performance.

10. Encourage trial and error

Encourage experimentation and innovative thought as a further means of developing responsible leadership abilities. Teams learn to assume responsibility for experimental gain and risk when given the freedom to experiment with a project's boundaries. Encouragement of experimentation also unintentionally encourages regular contact between team members, leaders, and other workers since experimenting involves communication within a team..

Chapter 6

Effective Leadership Techniques

Any company needs capable leadership to succeed. Effective team managers are necessary if you want to maximize production from your workforce. What, therefore, constitutes a great leader?

Although we've already discussed leadership traits, there is another factor that is equally crucial: leadership practices. But how do the two differ from one another?

A leader must have certain leadership behavioral traits, such as charm, confidence, and empathy. Leadership practices are the actions and tactics that leaders will use to consistently assist their team in becoming better versions of themselves and achieving progress.

The top leaders should actively engage in the following 12 leadership behaviors.

1. Mentoring connections

Good leaders will go above and above to provide training, support, and chances for their employees who demonstrate significant potential, even though a good workplace culture allows an opportunity for individuals to grow. A solid example of smart leadership practice is modifying your leadership approach to better suit your finest workers. Being a continuously strong and clear mentor and support system for employees is crucial, especially in this day and age when many workers are having trouble adjusting to remote work.

2. Encourage collaboration rather than just competition.

While some healthy rivalry among coworkers is not a terrible thing, it shouldn't be the only factor supervisors consider when evaluating personnel. An effective leadership strategy supports and promotes positive working relationships among the team. A strong bond between team members will promote teamwork and boost overall productivity.

3. Support career advancement for staff
When an individual progresses to the point where they can take on new responsibilities and a new job, a good leader is thrilled for them. While a leader typically does not aim for a high turnover of employees on his or her team, the succession of people and an improvement in the company's talent pool are seen as successes.

4. Take a chance on individuals (within reason)
Avoiding being restricted by predetermined boundaries is an excellent leadership habit. A strong leader, for instance, should be able to go beyond a candidate's educational background when hiring. Potential employees who have demonstrated their

ability to do challenging tasks in other contexts may prove to be valuable team members.

5. Constantly search for new talent

You shouldn't stop looking for new talent just because you don't need to fill a position right now. Being in contact with potential new hires is a smart leadership strategy since it's wise to have a fallback plan at all times. When you are next looking to fill a position, getting to know new people, learning about their abilities, and assessing how interested they might be in working with you in the future can be very helpful information to have. Given the exclusion many firms feel from their regular networks, networking may be difficult for some right now. However, this does not mean you should give up looking for fresh talent that will contribute to the long-term success of your company.

6. Publish your objectives.

Any excellent leader who genuinely wants to achieve should have a set of priorities that are prioritized and clearly stated. Making the team aware of your objectives and setting clear expectations for how each direct report will contribute to their execution are essential leadership skills. Employees can refer to your long-term goals as a leader if they're making choices that will have an impact on the business in the long run. They can also better comprehend why they're working so hard.

7. Provide immediate feedback

While annual reviews and more frequent ones are crucial, providing input right away can also be quite helpful. If something good is done, being praised right away will motivate someone to keep doing well. Similarly to this, seeing poor work early on makes it much simpler to repair and provide instruction on how to do so in the future. Staying consistent in your efforts to check in on your employees' progress and accomplishments, and to praise or offer constructive criticism as needed, will help keep them feeling more involved and appreciated, particularly when they are feeling stuck and isolated from their team while working from home.

8. An appreciation sandwich

The majority of people have heard of this leadership technique, and for good reason—it is still a highly effective way to assess an employee's performance. Essentially, it involves the leader praising or complimenting the employee for a job well done. Then comes criticism of something they didn't do as well or could improve upon, followed by yet another compliment. This is based on the notion that positive reinforcement makes it simpler to take criticism.

9. Evaluations based on the ideals of the company

Metrics alone make it simple to evaluate personnel, but they don't necessarily give the whole story. It's smart leadership practice to take the company's guiding principles into account when assessing an employee's performance. The saying "It's not only what you do, but how you act along the road" is frequently used to describe what it takes to be truly successful.

10. One-on-one interactions

One-on-ones are crucial in some circumstances, such as coaching, providing feedback, and even just checking in with a worker to see how they're doing. They enable you to establish closer relationships with each of your employees as a leader. Conversations between two people can reveal information that might not be seen in a group context. Additionally, it gives workers a chance to voice any worries they might have that they wouldn't want to discuss in a public context. When working remotely, setting up one-on-ones is not as difficult as some might believe. Despite not being in a shared workspace, you can check in with all of your employees frequently by using contemporary technology to make one-on-ones a regular part of your company calendar.

11. Brief, frequent gatherings to talk about concerns

Some unforeseen issues need more immediate attention than others and cannot wait for an annual, quarterly, or even weekly planned one-on-one review. Setting aside some time each day to discuss any concerns that are impacting the organization is a smart business practice. Depending on the situation, these sessions might be quick check-ins or extended discussions. These may be readily included in your work routines while working from home, much like one-on-ones. One of the most popular technologies in use today is virtual meetings and for good reason. Utilize the advantages of current technology and plan frequent, weekly virtual meetings with your staff to boost morale and promote advancement.

12. Have faith in your staff to execute the job.

Trusting your team to do the task you assign them is the finest leadership behavior you can have. The proper staff should be given the essential duties of leaders efficiently. Over time, trust must be developed, and it will depend on a worker's aptitude for the job at hand, their willingness to assume responsibility, their connections with coworkers, and other factors.

NOTE: Effective Leadership Techniques Have a Significant Impact

One must consider both excellent leadership practices and good leadership attributes when identifying what constitutes a good leader. The most effective leaders are confident enough to use the strategies required to maximize the performance of their employees.

Chapter 7

The Operational Procedures

Did you know that just 60% of employees claim to have a superior boss?

A capable manager may make a big contribution to the creation of a joyful and highly productive workplace. Your actions and leadership style can raise the morale of your direct reports and transform your group into a highly efficient one.

A few predefined great management concepts are followed by effective managers. If you haven't used them before, this article will explain their benefits as well as how to use them.

We'll go through 12 examples of good management and team-leading techniques, including everything from enhanced communication to the delegation and team-building activities. So let's get started.

1. Pick workers who you'd like to see in the hallway.

Poor recruiting has a big effect on a company's productivity and costs. They often perform worse than others, and managing a bad performer requires 70% more time than managing a good performer.

Additionally, if they don't agree with the company's philosophies, it will be challenging to have everyone rowing in the same direction. Profit maximization is the main goal.

Although a candidate must have the skills required for the job, you cannot "train" someone to have the right attitude and mindset for your company. Start by making things easier for yourself. Management of people is the management of a business.

There are several advantages to hiring employees who are a strong cultural fit.

These employees provide more value to your business. They are generally happy at work, and this enjoyment is reflected in their work performance.

Here are some steps you may take to improve your chances of finding the right applicant for the job.
- Consider a range of candidates.
- You need a large pool of potential employees to find the ideal fit. As long as you have assessment criteria in place, you will know who to choose and invite for an interview.

Furthermore, don't limit your search to a single job board since doing so will lessen your chances of finding the finest candidate. You never know, but professional social networking sites like AngelList and LinkedIn can be the key to connecting with prospective team members.

Establish Assessment Standards

Predetermined guidelines give the recruiting process more consistency. You may assess candidates, choose them for interviews, then compare and score interviewees' replies using your criteria. You may even go a step further than that since, according to a case study by Walden University, practical demonstrations are essential to determine if candidates are
1. qualified to do the position
2. a good match for the company.

First, think about cultural fit
Place more emphasis on cultural fit throughout the recruiting process than job fit. This means that when choosing a candidate, you must take into account more than just their qualifications.

You must establish if the prospect shares the ideas and values of your company before considering their skills and job fit.

If you saw them walking down the corridor, would you be happy to see them?

2. Act consistently throughout your actions
If you are consistent, your staff will know exactly what to expect from you, which stabilizes the workplace. The lack of a steady leader makes workers more prone to confusion and stress, both of which will lower output.

An excellent example of a consistent leader is Jack Welch, the former CEO of General Electric and usually considered one of history's greatest leaders.

To rate workers and terminate the poorest ones, Jack Welch utilized the "rank-and-yank" approach at General Electric.

Some people may have thought of him as having a severe leadership style, but he always behaved consistently and set clear standards.

Whether it's a good strategy or a terrible one, consistency provides many benefits for your organization.

Talk to other people (clearly, accurately, and thoroughly)
Inadequate management is typically the result of poor communication. If there are problems in your team, your communication skills may need to be improved.

For communication improvement, start with the basics. The receivers have no room for doubt thanks to the communication's clarity, precision, and thoroughness.

Transparency between management and employees

Additionally, it's important when you delegate tasks. Make sure to provide all necessary details while delivering instructions:

- Who is responsible for the task?
- what they must complete

When they must act, how should they act? (if needed)

The same principles hold for both written and spoken communication. Deliver the punchline first, and then provide details to support your primary argument.

Since listening is such an important component of effective communication, welcome any new inquiries from your team and be prepared to address them patiently and sympathetically.

Itd idea. It can damage your employee's confidence and self-esteem while making them defensive. Instead, find empty space or hold a one-to-one meeting in your office
.

Before you move on to any negative comments, begin with acknowledging the positives. If there are areas for improvement, talk with your staff about how you can achieve this together.

And when you come to share constructive feedback, be positive and informal. Your tone of voice is everything. It will help to take the fear out of a meeting and make your team member feel more relaxed.

Don't overwhelm them – use clear goals
Although it's important to stress areas that need improvement, there is a thing as too much information.

Instead of telling your employee about everything they need to work on, prioritize the most important area of concern for the moment and focus on that.

Once you address the most pressing issue, you can move on to the next thing.

Giving feedback can feel uncomfortable for both sides but it's crucial for employee's growth and thus—retention.

Paul Petrone, Linkedin's Head of Academic and Government Marketing, shares that employees are more likely to quit if they aren't growing in their role.

Regular feedback for your employees will help your day-to-day operations run more smoothly and give your team a sense of accomplishment as they develop and meet clear goals.

Consider introducing your team to benchmarking – comparing your methodologies to those of the best businesses in your industry. Doing so will provide a steady source of inspiration and motivation for dedicated workers.

Similarly, Key Performance Indicators – defined by your business objectives – were noted to improve industrial production. This is thanks to being able to compare KPIs with similar businesses to identify poor performance and locate improvement potential in your company.

8. Spread Your Positivity
Moods are contagious, and you have a bigger impact on everybody's mood than you may realize.

When you come to work in a bad mood, it affects the productivity, morale, and quality of work of your employees. So, don't forget, as a leader, you're responsible for setting the atmosphere throughout your company.

Now, this doesn't mean you have to hide negative things from your team, but if you act cranky and defeated , the chances are that attitude will spread to your team as well. So put any drama or panic to the side and act professionally.

To further spread positivity, you can:
Smile at team members and colleagues more
Celebrate the little wins with your team
Just as importantly, remember not to neglect mental health care for yourself either. Ensure that you get enough sleep, some exercise, eat a balanced diet, and take time out when you need to; otherwise, it will be hard to maintain a positive attitude.

If you feel you're close to burning out, request a personal day so you can return refreshed and positive, ready to motivate your team again. It's up to you as a good manager to manage your ups and downs.

9. Develop your people
When you focus on your staff's development, you're helping them to become better at their jobs. Helping them

learn more can parallelly improve their soft skills as well as specific job-related skills.

Developing Employees as Good Management Practice

If you want to encourage your team to grow and progress, you need to give them the resources they need to further their development. This means providing staff with:
- Training
- Mentoring
- Motivation

You can do that by getting staff more involved at work, such as mentoring a junior employee or presenting to senior staff. If you're used to hosting regular meetings, try setting a goal of each one directly benefiting as many employees as possible. Foster a learning environment.

Additionally, you can develop your team's skills by putting them into another role. This could be helping you to interview a prospective employee, working on a new project, or shadowing another colleague.

For new experiences outside of their day-to-day roles, see if your company has a professional development budget for sending employees to a training class.

Also, if there is an opportunity to bring an employee on a business trip or to a conference, go for it. Doing so will give your people the chance to see your company's work in the broader context of your industry or market.

They'll come back to work with renewed enthusiasm and a greater sense of purpose.

10. Be adaptable
Learn to let go of the urge to be in charge and practice being flexible with your team.

When you allow your employees to do jobs in a variety of ways (within the bounds of your business's rules), they are free to experiment and come up with more effective solutions.

The morale of your business might be negatively impacted by too tight management that alienates your staff. Remember that there are several approaches to completing a work, therefore be adaptable in your approach.

Being more patient also entails being more flexible. Some of your workers may first struggle to understand the details of a job. But they'll grow better, so give them some wiggle room in the meanwhile or let them find their path.

Once again, you should provide workers with enough training before granting them additional latitude. Before they can innovate, they must comprehend the essential business procedures.

Flexibility is something that effective managers should provide to staff members who are competent and secure in their positions. Give them additional chances to work through issues and discover answers with your help.

11. Be as open-minded as you can.
You may not realize how much your workforce values honesty and openness.

Transparency fosters trust, which in turn increases your staff's loyalty and respect.

Your team feels more confident when there is more openness. They are well aware of the direction the business is taking. Additionally, keeping staff members aware of potential issues reduces uncertainty and stress.

Effective Managers Foster Openness and Trust

There are other benefits as well when you are more transparent with your employees, including:

Teambuilding is expedited: Staff is more willing to share their ideas and express their concerns when a transparent approach is used.
The solution to issues gets simpler. Your workers may collaborate to develop solutions when they are aware of possible issues.
You create deeper connections: More open problem-solving fosters greater team trust and improves productivity at work. Therefore, everyone benefits.
Why aren't more leaders transparent if it is so important?

According to a Forbes article, managers are concerned about coming out as incompetent.

As a good management practice, transparency at work should be implemented since it has numerous positive effects.

12. Make judgments based on quantitative information

It is efficient to construct staff training and development programs using quantitative data. This method is also referred to as DDDM (data-driven decision-making.)

Top-performing businesses often use data to inform their choices. They prefer to follow the facts rather than wing it or follow their feelings. One of the well-known businesses that use data in the workplace is Google.

Data were used by training managers. Google first developed a list of traits that distinguish between effective managers and poor ones using information from employee polls.

They were able to redesign management training programs as a result of that realization, enabling new managers to succeed. However, your organization has to have a plan in place for a data-driven work culture. Define your objectives in the first phase, making sure they are attainable and quantifiable.

You'll be able to concentrate on the right areas and determine the kind of data you need to collect after you've defined your objectives.

There are benefits to using quantitative decision-making when developing new training programs, but you must also understand how to handle that data and, more critically, how to keep it safe.

Good leaders can handle any situation.

When you depend on solid management techniques, you may advance professionally and, as a result, advance your team.

Tend to the people, and the people will tend to the company, as John Maxwell once remarked regarding leadership.

To do this, you must set an example for people to follow and behave accordingly.

Display your humanity. Make it clear to your staff that you respect their work ethic and the outcomes they provide. Show compassion, empathy, and a helping hand when necessary.

Follow the 12 simple guidelines I provided in this book to improve your managing abilities and build a team that appreciates and trusts you.

Chapter 8

The Quarterly Dialogue

The quarterly dialogue is one of the management and leadership disciplines with the greatest potential for effect.

The comments and outcomes are evident after more than 15 years of teaching it to our customers. Due to the little amount of time, it takes (one hour every quarter, per direct report) and the results it generates, it has a strong effect. Results include concerns being resolved, increased communication, quicker progress, and, to mention a few, a stronger and healthier relationship between you and your direct report. The math is straightforward.

A one-on-one discussion lasting an hour is all that the quarterly dialogue entails once every 90 days with each of your direct reports. Each of you has the chance to discuss what's working and what isn't. It's simply a talk; it's not a performance evaluation.

So what's holding you back?

You could not want to hear about any more problems or offer individuals an opportunity to voice their complaints. As always, perhaps, the accompanying background may be helpful.

First and foremost, if you want to be a successful leader or manager, you must be aware of everything your direct reports consider to be problems (real or not).

Here is the setting. Any problems raised during the quarterly discussion will fall into one of three groups:

1. Issues that they must resolve: Ideally, you should delegate as many problems as you

can to your direct report for self-resolution. At this point, you need to mentor, coach, assist, and advise them on how to resolve the issue. This is your chance to foster independence rather than reliance on yourself.

2. Problems that are unsolvable Sincerity be damned, it was this main idea that inspired me to create Clarity Break. Most supervisors find these kinds of problems frustrating because they see them as complaining. You feel guilty or concerned because they can't be resolved to your direct report's satisfaction or because they don't like it but nothing is going to change. In a Quarterly Conversation, many of the topics on the list come under this heading. What you need to know about problems that can't be fixed or that won't change is as follows:

They just need a reply, resolution, or acknowledgment!

As a great manager or leader, you must master the art of stating something to the effect of, "I hear you, and I realize it's a problem that's driving you nuts. I want you to know that the problem you're describing exists for the reasons listed below [list the causes] and that it won't go away. Even if I am aware that you disagree, I only hope you can accept it.

You will sometimes let people down as a great manager or leader, therefore you must have the ability to handle disappointment. That knowledge will make you more resilient. In actuality, the Right People in the Right Seats will often respond with, "I understand and can live with it. I appreciate you listening.

The majority of the time, they come around and accept it, but sometimes they may stew for a long and you will have to put up with some pain for about a week. Because the issue cannot be resolved, the majority of poor leaders and managers postpone rather than responding or saying, "I'll get back to you on that," which irritates to grow. This causes a cloud of unsolved problems to hang over your relationship, dragging it down. And it's all because, in the majority of situations, you are trying to satisfy everyone and don't want to break the bad news.

Once again, all they need is a response.

3. Problems that need to be resolved There won't be many concerns in this third category after the other two have been clarified and dealt with. You will, unfortunately, have to deal with certain problems. However, the most important thing is to ensure that you address these problems as soon as possible. The finest thing you can do to get your direct report's respect and trust is to show it.

Schedule your quarterly meetings with your direct reports right away since it is one of the most effective leadership/management techniques we teach our customers. Take out your calendar and block out one hour every 30 days for the following 90 days for each direct report. You'll start to make great course adjustments and relationship enhancements. It's just going to become better and better.

I want to thank you all from the bottom of my heart for your dedication to the EOS cause. Your word-of-mouth and spreading the information to your peers have contributed significantly to our development.

Chapter 9

How to be your Own Boss

Want to work for yourself? I can relate.
Farrah Gray, a businesswoman, once said: "Construct your own goals, or someone else will employ you to build theirs." I remember reading that phrase when I was in my teens.

The remark stayed with me even though I was unaware of who Farrah Gray was.

Farrah Gray's Quote on Being Your own Boss
I reasoned that because so many individuals defied convention, forge their careers, and achieve success working for themselves, why couldn't I do the same?

I haven't worked a normal job in over ten years now.

I now work from wherever there is WiFi, make excellent money doing what I like, and have a very flexible schedule (I spent last year traveling across three continents).

Being your boss is fantastic, in my opinion.
How then do you become your own boss? Simply said, put in a lot of effort, study a lot, and persevere. All of our ambitions may come true, provided we have the confidence to follow them, as businessman Walt Disney famously stated.

I'll walk you through a 10-step plan in this post that outlines how to work from home as your own boss.

Let's start now.

Find out why you want to be your own boss in step one.
Why do you want to work for yourself?

The writer Christopher Morley once observed, "There is only one success: to be able to spend your life in your own manner."

This makes the issue in question very essential. So, how do you do it?

You may want to:
- Get paid more
- Make it possible for people to work and live anywhere in the globe.
- Create a flexible work schedule to provide more time for family time.
- Work in a job you like and are interested in.
- Follow your passion

Here's why it's important: Knowing your motivations for wanting to work for yourself can help you create your ideal life and then go about making it a reality.

Because 3 a.m. Zoom conversations from Indonesia aren't very enjoyable, you may want to steer clear of jobs that need you to be in the same time zone as your clients if you want to become a digital nomad.

In conclusion, having your own business has both benefits and drawbacks. Determine your top priorities and areas where you are willing to make concessions.

Christopher Morley Quote on How to Be Your Own Boss

2. Assess Your Situation and Your Capabilities

Knowing where you are will help you get where you're going.

So, evaluate.

What you should do is: In the beginning, assess your circumstance and how it will impact your capacity to be your own boss. For instance:

- Do you need to provide for a family?
- What are your monthly expenses?
- Do you have any emergency savings?
- Do you have any capital to put into your new company?

- How much time do you have to commit to being your own boss?
- What commitments (such as academics and raising children) take up the majority of your time?

Clarify your circumstances. Next, assess yourself:

- What talents do you possess?
- What are your advantages and disadvantages?
- Do you struggle to put off tasks until later?

You need to know what you're working with, so be honest with yourself.

Don't berate yourself, however.

Whatever your circumstances, you can change them and work for yourself. Start where you are, as tennis great Arthur Ashe said. Utilize your resources. Work your best.

Arthur Ashe's Quote on Being Your Own Boss

3. Prepare for the Change to Being Your Own Boss

The next step is figuring out how to go from working a job or going to school to becoming your own boss. Two primary paths exist:

Quit your work, put aside at least six months' worth of costs, and go all in.
Start a side business, and once it is profitable enough, leave your regular job.
If you're anything like me, you'll probably want to give it you're all. However, I can speak from personal experience when I say that this path may be quite difficult.

So think about launching a side business.

You will still have an income or studies to fall back on if you continue with your studies or career and things don't work out (and first attempts often don't).

4. Select a business plan

There are a ton of opportunities to "be your own boss."

But choosing a tried-and-true company plan when starting is beneficial; after all, why reinvent the wheel?

So here are three of the greatest methods to be your own boss without any money if you're seeking for "be your own boss ideas":

Do you have any services you might provide as a freelancer given your present skill set? One of the finest ways to be your own boss is via freelancing. Nevertheless, improving your abilities and earning more money may take some time.

Consulting and coaching: If you are knowledgeable about a subject, you may start your own business by selling your expertise. Additionally, after you've gained credibility, you may start selling information items.

E-commerce: If you're just starting a company, you might put up an online shop using a service like Shopify and work for yourself by selling goods. Additionally, dropshipping allows you to start selling things at no cost if you don't have any money to spend upfront.

How to Use Oberlo to Become Your Own Boss

5. Choose Your Market's Targets

Without clients, it is impossible to be your own boss.

Therefore, after deciding on a company plan, it's essential to pinpoint your target market—your ideal clients.

According to marketer Philip Kotler, "There is just one effective tactic. To precisely identify the target market and target it with a better product.

The first and most important piece of advice is to be a member of your target market.

Why? Simply put, selling something you wouldn't purchase yourself is harder. For instance, it would be difficult to connect to folks who buy cosmetics or hair products if you never use any of those things yourself. But if you're a watch enthusiast, it would be much simpler to advertise them thanks to your expertise and enthusiasm.

What then are your hobbies, passions, and interests? What area of expertise do you have? Use it to help you become your own boss, whatever that may be.

6. Identify a Challenge to Address (and Choose What to Sell)
You need to pinpoint an issue they have once you are aware of the sorts of individuals you might market to.

Every company deals with a problem:

- Cars are repaired by mechanics.
  Boredom is banished by TV

Now, the bigger and more painful the issue you address - and the better you solve it - the more money clients will give you. This is why sunglasses businesses enable individuals to express themselves and see better in sunny weather.

For instance, you may charge more for a dog harness when selling pet supplies than for a chew toy. Why? For an owner, a harness would be a better solution than a chew toy.

What issues does your intended audience have? What issues are you facing?

"If we attempted to think of a good concept, we wouldn't have been able to conceive of a decent idea," said Airbnb co-founder Brian Chesky. You just need to resolve a challenge in your own life.

Here's a summary of how to run your own business: Identify an issue, then market the solution.

7. Make Your Business Plan Clear
You ought to now have a straightforward business plan that you can use to start your own firm. What you need to know

The company structure who makes up your target market. What issue they are having. How do you propose to resolve their issue using your products or service
Here's an illustration:
Online goods dropshipping business model
Market segment: fashion-conscious young ladies
Problem: They seek novel means of expression and individuality.
Solution: Offer distinctive and striking gowns for sale online Now is the time to take action.

Get ready 8.

It's time to start construction and set up.

Before you spend your hard-earned money, it is now safer to generate some sales and ensure that your company concept is viable.

Therefore, only spend money when it is really necessary, and even then, limit it to a minimum. For instance:

need a website? Instead of spending money on a designer, use Shopify for free.
- Do you want to sell goods online? Don't buy stuff up front; instead, dropship using DSers.
- Desire to establish a home office? Rearrange your current furnishings before going to IKEA.
- Need to buy some equipment? For now, think about hiring or borrowing them.

Okay, it's time to decorate once you've moved in.

9. Create Your Company's Identity

Now for the enjoyable part: branding! However, you must establish your brand's identity before creating a logo.

Okay, but what precisely is a brand?

The CEO and creator of Amazon, Jeff Bezos, stated it best: "A company's brand is like a person's reputation."

By presenting your brand in the right manner, you may affect its reputation. The illustration below, for instance, demonstrates how colors and emotions are related, and how companies use this association to position their brands.

Be Your Own Boss: Color Psychology in Branding

What kind of brand will thus be most appealing to your target market? fun and groovy? Stylish and modern? brave and outgoing? basic and serene?

Whatever it is, give your brand some thought. Next, begin taking steps to become your own boss:

Using Shopify's company name generator, choose a name.
- Create a logo and identity for your social media accounts with Hatchful.
- Create and enhance social media profiles, such as a Facebook business page and an Instagram profile.

Keep in mind that you are still unsure about the viability of your company strategy.

Keep things simple and work swiftly; you can always make improvements afterward. Done is preferable to excellent, as Sheryl Sandberg, COO of Facebook, put it.

When you're ready, get some clients so you can start working for yourself!

10. Commence marketing to generate sales

The difficult thing now is attempting to make some sales to put your company to the test.

There are many strategies for marketing your goods or services, but some are better suited to a bootstrapped company.

Here are four online marketing strategies you may utilize to generate revenue and work for yourself:

1. Social media marketing: Engage with people individually and share material to attract your target market on social media platforms.

2. Direct outreach: Look through Instagram hashtags, Twitter profiles, and Facebook groups to locate potential customers. Next, establish a connection with them and inform them about your company.

3. Contact influencers whose following correspond to your target market to use influencer marketing. After that, collaborate

with them to market your service or product to their audience.

4. Paid promotion Run sponsored advertising campaigns on YouTube, Google, Facebook, and Instagram.

Good for you if you make some sales! Now is the moment to step up your marketing efforts.

However, what if you generate no sales? What you should do is:
- Examine your website to boost sales
- Boost your advertising
- Utilize social media to connect with members of your target market and get their opinions on your goods or services.

To a larger issue, find a better solution.

You may learn how to be your own boss if you have a solid strategy, put in the effort, and are persistent.

Being your own boss has numerous advantages, including more independence and the chance to work on a project you like. Your time is short, so don't squander it by living someone else's life, as Apple founder Steve Jobs famously stated.

In conclusion, here is a 10-step plan you may use to learn how to work for yourself:
1. Recognize your motivation for wanting to be your own boss.
2. Review your capabilities and position.
3. Make a plan to transition to becoming your own boss.
4. Pick a successful business strategy.
5. Determine your market segment
6. Find an issue to solve, then market the answer.
7. Establish the fundamentals of your company.
8. Make a brand that appeals to your target audience.
9. Create the infrastructure for your company, such as a website.

10. To generate revenue, begin promoting your product or service.

Finally, don't worry if your first effort fails. It merely means you need to try again; it doesn't mean you're a failure. Failure is only feedback, after all.

Types of Boss: Characteristics of Effective Bosses

Bosses are defined differently by different individuals, but in the management sense, a boss is someone who is in charge of other employees and accountable for the company's objectives and employee growth. Whatever a boss's responsibilities or management style, an effective boss definition focuses on making the most of each employee's unique skill set.

Are you looking for a job? Obtain employment.
What is a manager?

The brief definition of a boss is someone who has a supervisory position and is accountable for major tasks inside a business or organization. The term "boss" may also apply to a person who is in charge of hiring, developing, and training staff members as well as making sure that departmental tasks are accomplished and objectives are fulfilled.

The boss is often the final decision-maker within a department and is essential to the success of the whole company. For these reasons, managers must be ready for their professional futures.

Making significant choices that affect every employee in a certain department is a serious responsibility. For this reason, a lot of managers study books and articles and register for courses on leadership and different management styles.

Bosses should work to build these critical competencies while considering how to enhance their performance:

Problem-solving: Managers need to be adept at this skill. This comprises the capacity to not just identify issues and their solutions, but also to establish the existence of problems in the first place.

Time management: Bosses are in charge of both their time management and ensuring time for others. Bosses that have good time management techniques often maintain high levels of output and morale.

Empathy: Even though it may not seem like the most logical management skill to have, demonstrating empathy often shows to be crucial for managers who interact with workers. It exhibits high levels of emotional intelligence and the capacity to attend to the needs of others.

Decision-making: Effective decision-making abilities are closely tied to problem-solving on the essential list of management attributes. They also make for good bosses. The top managers can make choices quickly and effectively and carry them out either on their own or with the help of other employees.

3 managerial techniques used by bosses

Although there are many different kinds of bosses, three management styles primarily influence a boss's management approach. Which are:

Authoritarian

An autocratic manager is frequently referred to as such. Since they tend to penalize bad behavior to stop it and reward good behavior, autocratic managers may be quite successful in how they handle disagreements and poor behavior.

Although an authoritarian boss like Steve Jobs, for example, may not always be the nicest, in the right setting they may be an inspirational visionary with high expectations that all workers must meet.

Because of this, some managers find autocratic leadership to be a successful style.

Democratic
A democratic leader is ready to solicit feedback from their workforce. These managers that prioritize leadership are more likely to schedule meetings to discuss current projects and efforts at work.

Democratic leaders tend to seek to empower their team to participate in the decision-making process because they are collaborative people who understand the value of delegating and how to execute it properly. When given the right backing by employers, these CEOs often build cohesive teams with high levels of productivity.

Laissez-faire
Laissez-faire leadership is a hands-off style of management that offers staff members complete freedom to act whenever they like. It is regarded as the least successful of the

three management styles. Strong laissez-faire leaders often check in with their staff to monitor objective progress and make sure people under their supervision have the resources necessary to finish initiatives.

However, sometimes, ineffective laissez-faire leaders fail to check in at all, and as a result, the output and business culture become entirely reliant on the attitudes and skills of the workforce.

Frequently Asked Questions about Bosses
You may improve as a boss by learning the responses to the following often-asked questions:

How should managers solicit input from their staff?
Small firms must foster a culture where employee input is welcomed rather than feared if they want to get candid feedback from their staff. The democratic leadership style that includes workers in certain

important workplace choices is often conducive to this kind of culture. Bosses may then solicit input from employees during meetings by offering anonymous channels for the receipt and analysis of employee comments, issues, and inquiries.

How do I decide which management approach to use?
Choosing the best management style requires taking into account your personality, leadership style, and working environment. For instance, an authoritarian leadership style may work best for you if you make better judgments on your own or after consulting only close friends and family. A democratic leadership style also offers an opportunity to get insight and ideas from your workers provided you place a high emphasis on feedback and guidance. Laissez-faire leadership may suit your needs if you have a lot of faith in your employees or operate a company in an industry where self-starters are popular.

What characteristics make a good boss?

Good employers give their workers authority. Good bosses encourage employees to perform at their highest level by taking on the roles of mentor, coach, and even buddy, and they provide them with the opportunity to advance into leadership positions should they so choose. Good bosses are encouraging and concerned for the well-being of their subordinates, and they express gratitude for a job well done, which raises team spirit. When failures are unavoidable, they also discuss their personal experiences. Most importantly, successful managers make it easier for workers by treating everyone fairly and ensuring that everyone gets the resources they need to thrive.

Chapter 10

Taking the Helm

Summary. The author has spent more than ten years researching how top performers make the move to management. As businesses grow leaner and...

Even for the most talented people, being a leader is a challenging but worthwhile road of ongoing learning and self-development. Being your first boss is the essential first challenge on the journey, although we often ignore it. That's unfortunate since the struggles encountered throughout this rite of passage have far-reaching effects on both the person and the organization.

Executives' initial managerial roles have a permanent impact on them. Years later, many look back on those early months as transformative times that shaped their leadership ideas and approaches in ways that may haunt and limit them for the rest of their lives. When a person who has been promoted due to outstanding individual performance and credentials fails to succeed in adjusting to managerial duties, organizations incur significant human and financial costs.

Given how challenging the change is, the failures shouldn't come as a surprise. Ask any senior executive to remember how they felt as new managers. Ask any new management about their first few months as a boss. If you get an honest response, you will learn about someone's perplexity and, for some, tremendous disorientation. The new position didn't feel at all like it should. It seemed to be too much for one person to manage. In addition, whatever its purview, it had nothing to do with leadership.

Do you realize how difficult it is to be the boss when you are so out of control, said one new branch manager at a financial firm? Verbalizing it is challenging. It's the emotion you experience after having a kid. You are still without a kid on day X minus 1. You suddenly become a mother or a father on day X, and you're expected to be an expert at raising children.

It's remarkable how little attention has been given to new managers' experiences and the difficulties they encounter, given the importance and difficulty of this initial leadership exam. Books discussing strong and successful leaders are stacked high on the shelf. However, few discuss the difficulties of learning to lead, particularly for new managers.

I've researched persons making significant career transitions to management for the last 15 years or more, concentrating in particular on the star performer who gets promoted to manager. My first goal was to provide new managers with a platform to discuss what it means to learn to manage in their own words. I originally kept track of 19 new managers over their first year to acquire a unique peek into their perspective: What did they find the most challenging? They needed to learn what, though? What method did they use to learn it? What tools did they use to master their new tasks and make the transition easier?

Since publishing Becoming a Manager in its initial edition in 1992, I have carried out more research on the changes a person goes through when they become a manager. I've created and directed new-manager leadership programs for businesses and not-for-profit organizations. I've authored case studies regarding new managers in many roles and sectors. New managers have described a transition that is becoming more difficult as businesses have become leaner and more dynamic, with various units collaborating to offer integrated products and services and businesses forming a variety of strategic alliances with suppliers, clients, and rival businesses.

I want to be clear that the challenges these new managers encounter are the rule, not the exception. These managers are not dysfunctional ones working in dysfunctional companies. They are regular folks with typical adjustment issues. The great majority of them make it through the change and figure out how to do their new duties. If the shift was less traumatic, though, consider how much more successful they would be.

We must assist new managers in comprehending the fundamental essence of their position—what it means to be in charge—to help them pass this first leadership exam. Most people identify as managers and leaders; they speak in terms of leadership; and they undoubtedly bear the responsibilities of that role. Yet they just fail to grasp it.

Why Managing is So Difficult to Learn

One of the first things that newly appointed managers learn is that their position, which is by definition a stretch assignment, is considerably more difficult than they had imagined. They are shocked to discover that there is a disconnect between their present skill set and the criteria of the new job, as well as between the approaches and talents necessary for success in individual contributor and management roles.

Success in their previous positions was mostly based on their abilities and deeds. Since their careers as individual performers did not qualify them for managing a team, they are now in charge of creating and carrying out the agenda for the whole organization.

Consider Michael Jones, the newly hired branch manager of the securities business I just described. (Persons referenced in this article have had their identities concealed.) Michael was a top producer, one of the most aggressive and creative brokers in his area, and had been a broker for 13 years. No one at his firm was shocked when the regional director invited him to think about a management career since new branch managers were often promoted from the ranks based on individual skills and accomplishments. Michael was certain that he knew what it takes to be a successful manager. In reality, he had often said that if he had been in charge, he would have been ready and able to make improvements and make life in the branch better. But after a month in his new position, he was experiencing significant panic attacks since putting his ideas into action was more challenging than he had anticipated. He concluded that there was no going back after he had renounced his "security blanket."

Although it surprises him, Michael's response is not rare. Learning by doing is how one develops leadership skills. It is impossible to teach it in a classroom. It is a skill that is largely learned via practical experience gained while working, particularly in challenging circumstances when the new manager works outside his comfort zone and learns by doing. Since they haven't made many blunders before, most famous performers are unfamiliar with this. Few managers are also aware that they are learning during challenging, error-prone periods. Gradually and slowly, learning takes place.

A new professional identity evolves as this process progressively moves forward—as the new manager unlearns a mindset and practices that have helped him during a very successful early career. He learns new methods to define success and find fulfillment in his job, internalizes new ways of thinking and being, and finds new ways to measure accomplishment. This kind of psychological adjustment is demanding, as expected. I never realized a promotion could be so difficult, says one new boss.

unpleasant and painful. Will I enjoy management? and "Will I be excellent at management?" are inevitable thoughts for new managers. Of course, there are no quick fixes; only experience can provide them. And a third, more uncomfortable question is often added to these two: "Who am I becoming?"

A New Manager's Fallacies

It's challenging to become a boss, but I don't want to create an unrelentingly depressing image. In my study, I have discovered that new managers' preconceptions about their roles often make the transition more difficult than it has to be. Some of what they believe managers should do is true. However, since these ideas are oversimplified and unfinished, they lead to erroneous expectations that people find difficult to reconcile with the realities of management life. New managers have a far better chance of succeeding if they acknowledge the following myths, some of which are so widely accepted that they virtually qualify as myths. See the exhibit "Why New Managers Don't Get It" for a comparison of the myths and the facts.

Why New Managers Fail to Understand It Beginning managers sometimes struggle in their new positions, at least at first, because they have preconceived notions or beliefs about what it takes to be a manager. These fallacies encourage new managers to ignore crucial leadership tasks because they are oversimplified and uncompleted.

Managers exercise a lot of power.
New managers often concentrate on the perks of being the boss when asked to explain their work. They believe that because of their new position, they will have more power and, therefore, greater flexibility and independence to act as they see fit for the company. They won't be

"burdened by the ridiculous expectations of others," in the words of one.

New managers who hold this belief are in for a nasty shock. Those I have researched report that interdependencies have encircled them rather than giving them greater power. They experience a sense of constraint rather than freedom, particularly if they were used to a star performer's relative independence. They are caught up in a web of connections with coworkers, superiors, peers, and others within and outside the business, all of whom put constant and sometimes contradictory demands on them. The outcome is a stressed-out, disjointed daily routine.

One new boss asserts, "The reality is that you have no control over anything." "I feel like I'm not performing my job, which is to be with the people, since the only time I feel in control is when I lock my door," the speaker said. "It's humbling that someone who works for me may get me fired," says another new boss.

The individuals who don't come under a new manager's official jurisdiction are the ones who are most likely to make her life unpleasant, such as outside suppliers or supervisors in another division. A rising star at a chemical firm Sally McDonald accepted a job in product development with great expectations, perfect credentials as an individual performance, a thorough understanding of the company's culture, and even the purported wisdom from a leadership development course. Three weeks later, she made the somber observation: "Being a manager is not the same as being the boss. It has to do with being held, prisoner. This group is filled with terrorists that want to abduct me.

Becoming a manager, not a boss, is how one disillusioned new leader puts it. It has to do with taking hostages.

New managers won't be able to lead successfully until they abandon the fantasy of authority for the reality of negotiating interdependencies. As we've seen, controlling the environment in which the team works is more than just overseeing the direct report team. The team won't have the resources required to do its work unless it can identify and establish productive connections with the important individuals on whom it relies.

Even when new managers recognize the value of these connections, they often disregard or dismiss them in favor of what appears to be the more pressing responsibility of managing people who are physically near to them: their subordinates. When they do embrace their network-building job, they often experience stress from its expectations. Additionally, it becomes tiring to negotiate with these other parties from a position of relative weakness, which is often the situation faced by new managers at the bottom of the hierarchy.

But there are significant benefits to controlling interdependencies. Winona Finch created a business plan for the introduction of a Latin American version of the firm's American adolescent magazine while working in business development for a major U.S. media corporation. Finch requested to oversee the project once it received provisional permission. She and her team had to overcome several challenges. Top management did not support international ventures, and before receiving final finance, Finch would have to sign contracts with local distributors who represented 20% of the Latin American market. This would be a difficult assignment for an unproven newspaper vying for limited newsstand space. Her business would have to depend on the sales team of the company's main women's magazine in Spanish, who were used to selling a quite different sort of product, to keep expenses under control.

Winona had previously worked as an acting manager for two years, so despite the deluge of details she had to handle while establishing the new business, she was aware of how crucial it was to devote time and focus to managing relationships with her superiors and colleagues. For instance, she prepared executive notes from her department heads every two weeks and sent them to executives at the corporate level. She established frequent Latin American board meetings where senior global executives from both the adolescent and women's magazines could review regional strategies to improve communication with the women's magazine.

Despite her previous management expertise, she experienced the normal difficulties that new managers face: "It's like you have final examinations every day of the year," she says. Even Nevertheless, the revised version was released on time and performed better than anticipated in the business plan.

From the manager's position, authority flows.
Don't get me wrong: New managers do have some influence despite the interdependencies that limit them. The issue is that the majority of them incorrectly think that their official authority, which comes with their increasingly lofty—well, comparatively speaking—position in the hierarchy, is what gives them their power. Many individuals choose a direct, authoritarian style as a consequence of this underlying presumption, not because they are eager to utilize their newfound authority over others but rather because they think it would provide the best results.

However, new managers quickly discover that direct subordinates don't always comply when instructed to do something. A subordinate is less likely to simply obey commands the more competent she is. When questioned, some new managers acknowledge that they weren't always listening to their superiors.

After a few traumatic encounters, new managers get the disturbing conclusion that "everything except" formal authority is the source of their power. In other words, power only develops when the manager builds trust among peers, superiors, and subordinates. One manager I saw recalled, "It took me three months to realize I had no impact on many of my workers. It was as if I was speaking to myself.

How tough it is to gain people's respect and trust surprises many new managers. The fact that their experience and track record don't speak for themselves shocks and even offends them. According to my study, many people are likewise unaware of the factors that influence believability.

They must exhibit their moral character—the desire to perform honorably. This is especially crucial for subordinates, who often scrutinize every word and nonverbal cue in search of clues about the new boss's intentions. Such observation might be unsettling. One new boss adds, "I knew I was a decent person, and I sort of expected people to embrace me instantly for who I was." But people were cautious, so you had to earn it.

They must exhibit their skill by acting morally soundly. This may be an issue since at the beginning, new managers feel the need to demonstrate their technical expertise and skill, which are the cornerstones of their success as individual performers. Technical prowess is crucial for earning the respect of subordinates, but direct reports aren't searching for it as their main competency.

Peter Isenberg led a team of senior, experienced traders when he assumed control of a trading desk at a major investment bank. He used a hands-on approach to building his reputation by recommending traders to liquidate specific holdings or test out new trading techniques. The dealers retaliated by pressing for an explanation of each direction. Things started to feel awkward. The dealers' replies to the remarks made by their new boss were sour and abrupt. Isenberg, who was aware of his ignorance of overseas markets, asked one of the more senior individuals a straightforward inquiry about pricing one day. The trader volunteered to continue the conversation at the end of the day after pausing his work for several minutes to explain the situation. People at the desk started teaching me about the work after I stopped talking all the time and started listening, and, importantly, they seemed to question my calls far less, according to Isenberg.

The new manager had lost his credibility as a manager and leader because he was so anxious to demonstrate his technical proficiency. His readiness to step up and attempt to fix issues aroused underlying concerns about his management ability. He was seen by the traders as a "control freak" and micromanager who didn't merit their respect.

Finally, new managers must exhibit influence—the capacity to provide and carry out the proper action. A firsthand report of one of the new managers I looked at claims that there is "nothing worse than working for a powerless boss." Because new managers are the "small bosses" of the company, as I've said, it might be challenging to gain and exercise authority inside it. One new manager claims, "I felt on top of the world when I learned I was finally being promoted." "I got the impression that I would soon reach the summit of the ladder I had been clambering up for years. Then, all of a sudden, I felt like I was back at the beginning, except this time it wasn't even apparent which rungs I was on or where I was going.

Once again, we see a new manager make the mistake of putting too much faith in his official power to exert influence. Instead, he has to develop a web of solid, mutually beneficial connections inside his team and the whole firm, one strand at a time, to increase his influence.

Direct reports must be under management's supervision.
Most new managers want conformity from their colleagues, in part due to uncertainty in a foreign job. They worry that their direct reports will dominate them if they don't establish this early on. They often depend excessively on their official power to achieve this control—a strategy whose efficacy is, as we have shown, at best debatable.

However, even if they are successful in exerting some level of control, whether, via official authority or power acquired through time, they will have won a deceptive triumph. Compliance does not imply dedication. People won't take the initiative if they aren't dedicated. Additionally, the manager cannot successfully delegate if staff members aren't taking the initiative. The direct reports are unwilling to take the calculated risks that result in the ongoing change and improvement that are necessary for the challenging business climate of today.

Winona Finch, who oversaw the adolescent magazine's introduction to Latin America, was aware that she faced a commercial task that would need the cooperation of her whole staff. She had been given the position in part due to her unique personality, which her supervisors believed would make up for her lack of prior expertise in the Latin American market and handling profit-and-loss duties. She had a reputation for being a clear thinker and was also pleasant and approachable. She used these inherent skills to construct her leadership philosophy and style throughout the project.

She used influence instead of formal authority to obtain what she needed from her team by fostering a culture of inquiry. People felt empowered, engaged, and responsible for achieving the company's mission throughout the organization as a consequence. Winona was laid-back and enjoyable, according to a subordinate. But to find out more, she would keep asking questions. She would repeat everything you said back to her, making sure that everyone understood exactly what you were saying. You have to be consistent after she had the facts and realized what you were doing. You told me X; why are you doing Y? she would ask. I'm perplexed." She was demanding, but she didn't insist that everyone do things the way she wanted. Because they were given the authority to accomplish the team's objectives rather than being given orders to do so, her subordinates were devoted to them.

The more authority managers are ready to provide their staff in this manner, the more influence they are likely to have. They establish their managerial credibility when they choose a leadership style that encourages initiative from their team members.
Managers should concentrate on developing strong personal connections.
Building trust, influence, and mutual expectations with a broad range of individuals are necessary for new managers to manage interdependencies and exercise informal authority derived from personal credibility. This is often accomplished through developing fruitful interpersonal connections. But ultimately, the new manager has to learn how to unleash the potential of a group. Simply concentrating

on developing personal connections with team members might sabotage that process.

Many new managers fail to acknowledge, much less deal with, their team-building obligations within their first year of employment. Instead, they mistakenly equate managing their team with managing the team members, seeing their people-management duty as developing the best possible connections with each subordinate.

They give little to no thought to the culture and performance of the team, focusing instead on individual performance. They barely ever use discussion boards to find and fix issues. Some people spend an excessive amount of time with a select group of dependable subordinates, often those who seem to be most helpful. Even though a problem affects the whole team, new managers often tackle it one-on-one. As a result, they end up making judgments based on unduly scarce knowledge.

Roger Collins was asked for the location of an allocated parking space that had just become available by a subordinate during his first week on the job as a sales manager for a Texas software business. Collins, hoping to establish a strong rapport with the seasoned salesperson who had worked for the firm for years, said, "Sure, why not?" Within an hour, a different salesperson who made a lot of money barged into Collins' office and threatened to resign. The shaded parking space seems to have been sought after for practical and symbolic reasons, and Collins's casual gesture was received negatively by many people. The celebrity couldn't understand the manager's choice.

Collins finally resolved what he saw to be a minor management issue—"This is not the kind of thing I'm supposed to be thinking about," he said—but he soon realized that every choice he made about a team member had an impact on that person. He had been operating on the presumption that his whole team would run well if he could build strong relationships with everyone who reported to him. He discovered that managing each person was different from managing the collective. In my study, I often hear new managers talk about instances when they made an exception for one subordinate—typically to build a good connection with that person—but later regretted it due to the unexpectedly detrimental effects on the team. For rising stars who have done a lot on their own, it might be particularly challenging to understand this idea.

I often hear rookie managers mention circumstances when they made an exception for one employee but afterward regretted it due to the team's unanticipated negative effects.

When rookie managers just concentrate on one-on-one interactions, they overlook a crucial component of successful leadership: using the group's collective strength to boost individual performance and commitment. A leader may unleash the problem-solving power of the team's various skills by influencing the team culture—the group's norms and values.

Managers are responsible for ensuring orderly operations.
Like many management myths, this one is somewhat accurate but deceptive since it only communicates a portion of the truth. An organization's seamless functioning requires a manager to constantly juggle a large number of tasks, which is a very challenging undertaking. Indeed, a young manager's time and effort might be completely consumed by the intricacy of sustaining the status quo.

However, new managers must also understand that they must suggest and start improvements that will improve the performance of their teams. This often entails criticizing organizational practices or systems that operate outside of their official sphere of power, which most people find surprising. They won't start taking their leadership duties seriously until they fully grasp this aspect of the job. Oh, and don't forget to set yourself up for success.

This broader view benefits the organization as well as the new manager. Organizations must continually revitalize and transform themselves. They can meet these challenges only if they have cadres of effective leaders capable of both managing the complexity of the status quo and initiating change.

It's Not Just New Managers
Learning to identify the myths I've just described will give new managers a significant edge as they navigate the

challenging process of becoming a boss. However, given the complexity of their new duties, they will inevitably make errors as they attempt to piece together the management jigsaw. Making mistakes is never enjoyable, regardless of how crucial they are to the learning process. As their professional identities are distorted and twisted, they will experience agony. They will often feel alone as they work to adapt to a new position.

Sadly, my study has revealed that not many new managers seek assistance. This is partly a result of yet another myth: The boss is meant to know everything, therefore asking for assistance is a certain indication that a new manager is a "promotion error." Experienced managers are aware that nobody has all the solutions. A manager does get insights with time and experience. Furthermore, having access to the support and guidance of peers and superiors makes it simpler to learn on the job, as several studies have shown.

Another reason new managers don't seek assistance is that they worry about the risks of developing collaborative connections, which are sometimes more hypothetical than actual. You run the danger of having others use your fears, errors, and flaws against you if you discuss them with colleagues in your division of the company. The same is true when discussing your issues with your supervisor. The inherent tension between the evaluator and developer positions is an ancient conundrum. As a result, gaining assistance requires creativity from new management. For instance, they could look for peers who are in another organization entirely or outside of their area or job. While the issue with bosses is tough to resolve precisely, it can be mitigated. And this is a lesson that applies to both young managers and seasoned bosses.

Because she views her immediate supervisor as a danger rather than an ally in her growth, the new manager avoids asking her for help. Even when she is in severe need of assistance, she refuses to ask for it because she worries about being punished for errors and failures. According to a new manager:

I am aware that my manager should be my primary point of contact since that is what he is there for. He knows, thus I probably owe it to him to approach him and explain the situation. He most likely has some sound recommendations. But sharing with him is not safe. He is an unproven individual. He can lose trust in you and believe that things aren't going well if you probe too much. He could think you're a little out of control, in which case your task becomes really difficult. He'll ask a lot of questions about what you're doing down there right away, and before you know it, he'll be participating right in the midst of it.

That is an awkward scenario. I wouldn't turn to him if I needed assistance.

Many times, these worries are valid. Many new managers have come to regret their efforts to establish a mentoring bond with their boss. One of them adds, "I don't dare to pose a question that may be seen as naïve or foolish." "Once I asked him a question, and he treated me in the business like a kindergartener. He seemed to be saying, "That was the silliest thing I've ever seen." What on earth were you thinking?

This is a chance that was sadly missed by the boss, the new manager, and the company as a whole. It implies that the employer of the new manager forfeits the opportunity to shape the manager's early ideas and preconceptions about her new role and how she should approach it. The opportunity for the new manager to access organizational resources—from financial resources to knowledge of senior management's priorities—that the superior might most effectively deliver is lost.

It may make all the difference when a new manager can establish a solid working connection with his boss, but perhaps not in the manner the new management anticipates. According to my study, nearly half of the rookie managers ultimately ask their supervisors for help, often due to an impending crisis. Many people are pleased to learn that their bosses are more understanding of their inquiries and errors than they had anticipated. One new manager remembers, "He knew that I was still in the learning process and was more than happy to assist in any way he could."

A little over half of rookie managers ask their employers for help. Many people are pleased to learn that their bosses are more understanding of their inquiries and errors than they had anticipated.

Even the most knowledgeable instructors can seem to be too detached. According to one manager, she learned from a direct superior: "She is demanding, but she has a reputation for developing people and supporting them, not throwing them to the wolves. But after the first 60 days, I wasn't sure. She didn't offer it's Not Just New Managers

Learning to identify the myths I've just described will give new managers a significant edge as they navigate the challenging process of becoming a boss. However, given the complexity of their new duties, they will inevitably make errors as they attempt to piece together the management jigsaw. Making mistakes is never enjoyable, regardless of how crucial they are to the learning process. As their professional identities are distorted and twisted, they will experience agony. They will often feel alone as they work to adapt to a new position.

Sadly, my study has revealed that not many new managers seek assistance. This is partly a result of yet another myth: The boss is meant to know everything, therefore asking for assistance is a certain indication that a new manager is a "promotion error." Experienced managers are aware that nobody has all the solutions. A manager does get insights with time and experience. Furthermore, having access to the support and guidance of peers and superiors makes it simpler to learn on the job, as several studies have shown.

Another reason new managers don't seek assistance is that they worry about the risks of developing collaborative connections, which are sometimes more hypothetical than actual. You run the danger of having others use your fears, errors, and flaws against you if you discuss them with colleagues in your division of the company. The same is true when discussing your issues with your supervisor. The inherent tension between the evaluator and developer positions is an ancient conundrum. As a result, gaining assistance requires creativity from new management. For instance, they could look for peers who are in another organization entirely or outside of their area or job. While the issue with bosses is tough to resolve precisely, it can be mitigated. And this is a lesson that applies to both young managers and seasoned bosses.

Because she views her immediate supervisor as a danger rather than an ally in her growth, the new manager avoids asking her for help. Even when she is in severe need of assistance, she refuses to ask for it because she worries about being punished for errors and failures. According to a new manager:

I am aware that my manager should be my primary point of contact since that is what he is there for. He knows, thus I probably owe it to him to approach him and explain the situation. He most likely has some sound recommendations. But sharing with him is not safe. He is an unproven individual. He can lose trust in you and believe that things aren't going well if you probe too much. He could think you're a little out of control, in which case your task becomes really difficult. He'll ask a lot of questions about what you're doing down there right away, and before you know it, he'll be participating right in the midst of it. That is an awkward scenario. I wouldn't turn to him if I needed assistance.

Many times, these worries are valid. Many new managers have come to regret their efforts to establish a mentoring bond with their boss. One of them adds, "I don't dare to pose a question that may be seen as naïve or foolish." "Once I asked him a question, and he treated me in the business like a kindergartener. He seemed to be saying, "That was the silliest thing I've ever seen." What on earth were you thinking?

This is a chance that was sadly missed by the boss, the new manager, and the company as a whole. It implies that the employer of the new manager forfeits the opportunity to shape the manager's early ideas and preconceptions about her new role and how she should approach it. The opportunity for the new manager to access organizational resources—from financial resources to knowledge of senior management's priorities—that the superior might most effectively deliver is lost.

It may make all the difference when a new manager can establish a solid working connection with his boss, but perhaps not in the manner the new management anticipates. According to my study, nearly half of the rookie managers ultimately ask their supervisors for help, often due to an impending crisis. Many people are pleased to learn that their bosses are more understanding of their inquiries and errors than they had anticipated. One new manager remembers, "He knew that I was still in the learning process and was more than happy to assist in any way he could."

A little over half of rookie managers ask their employers for help. Many people are pleased to learn that their bosses are more understanding of their inquiries and errors than they had anticipated.

Even the most knowledgeable instructors can seem to be too detached. According to one manager, she learned from a direct superior: "She is demanding, but she has a reputation for developing people and supporting them, not throwing them to the wolves. But after the first 60 days, I wasn't sure. She didn't offer to assist, and I was so upset since everything was so difficult. I was going crazy about it. She asked me a question after I asked her one. I received no replies. Then I realized what she wanted. She would discuss my options with her after I entered with some preconceived notions of how I would handle the circumstance. She would be with me all the time in the world.

His story poignantly illustrates the need for new managers' employers to comprehend—or just remember—how challenging it is to take on a management post for the first time. The benefits of assisting a new manager in succeeding extend beyond that person. The performance of the new manager is critical to the overall success of the company. to assist, and I was so upset since everything was so difficult. I was going crazy about it. She asked me a question after I asked her one. I received no replies. Then I realized what she wanted. She would discuss my options with her after I entered with some preconceived notions of how I would handle the circumstance. She would be with me all the time in the world.

His story poignantly illustrates the need for new managers' employers to comprehend—or just remember—how challenging it is to take on a management post for the first time. The benefits of assisting a new manager in succeeding extend beyond that person. The performance of the new manager is critical to the overall success of the company.

www.ingramcontent.com/pod-product-compliance
Lightning Source LLC
Chambersburg PA
CBHW052356220526
45465CB00003BB/1130